LET GO, LET GOD

—LOOK AT ME NOW—

Be free. Live in peace. You have purpose!

DR. KERRIEL V. LYLES

DR. K

ISBN 979-8-88832-646-6 (paperback)
ISBN 979-8-88832-647-3 (digital)

Christian Faith Publishing
832 Park Avenue
Meadville, PA 16335
www.christianfaithpublishing.com

Printed in the United States of America

My grandma lived to see me graduate with my bachelor's degree from the University of Southern Mississippi. I had just started my master's program when she passed away fourteen years ago. It is so much that she has missed, and I wished she was here with me. Oh, I miss her dearly.

I dedicate everything I do to you, Grandma. I hope I am making you proud.

Uncle Slim, you were twenty-five years old when you passed. You hadn't really started living. So I dedicate everything I do to you. I am living out of my dreams for you since your life was taken too soon.

ACKNOWLEDGMENTS

My daughter, you are one of my main inspirations. I love you dearly. You have helped me become the person I am today.

My godson, I am so proud of you. You are amazing. I love you dearly.

My best friend, you are the most selfless person I know. I love you, sister.

God has brought some special people into my life. You know who you are. I am big on giving you your flowers now, so you can enjoy them and know how much you are appreciated. Thank you for being a part of my life.

INTRODUCTION

I Am Beautifully Broken!

It is easy to cry out, "Life is not fair!" "Why do I have to fight all my life?" "How come this is the life I was dealt?" But then I realized, why not me? No, life is not fair, but the choice to have a better life is up to me. I understood that a new anointing has come upon me and I will never miss again because I have been called to be a spiritual sniper. And it is not about the life we are dealt but how you still win in the midst of it all.

From ashes to beauty, and still, I stand! I stand because I surrendered to God. My life was falling to pieces in my hands, so when I released control, the pieces came together. See, the process does not feel good, and it definitely does not look good, but God. When you endure the process, that means you are trusting God to get you through it.

Never believe you are supposed to go through things alone. That's what the devil wants you to believe. When you go through things alone, you get depressed, you are confused, and negative thoughts take over your mind. But when you go through things with someone, not just anybody. Someone who can motivate, encourage, and uplift you. God will bring you around the right person or people, but you must have the discernment to understand who is there to help you or to deceive you.

Throughout my life, God has brought many people who were there for a season or who are currently in my life. Many people in your life serve a purpose of why they are in your life, but only you can figure that out.

So this book is to empower you to let go, let God, and walk in your purpose!

A previous spiritual leader in my life shared this with me:

> He heals the brokenhearted and binds
> up their wounds. (Psalm 147:3)

Let go of the idea of perfection. You are not perfect. You are real. Let yourself be flawed, and allow yourself to make mistakes. Recognize that you are not always going to have it all together. Sometimes, your heart is going to break. You are going to get hurt. You are going to feel pain. Do not apologize for being broken. Every crack tells you a little more about yourself, your strength, your courage, and your tenacity, what you are made of. Do not hide these pieces from the world. That is a part of who you are. The most beautiful people are the ones whose hearts are heavy because they love the deepest. They have seen the dark and appreciate everything that shines. They are compassionate, understanding, and empathetic. Beautiful hearts do not just happen; they are made. You, my dear, are going to show the world just how beautiful you are.

This resonated with me deeply because this is me! I am a walking testimony! We go through things in life, good and bad. We are to share our experiences with others. Because most of the time, we are not going through things for ourselves. We are witnesses unto the world, letting people know that God is real! Anything is possible with God!

Are you ready to be encouraged? Open up your heart and mind to receive. You are reading this for a reason. As I share my story, reevaluate your life. As you look at yourself in the mirror, what do you see? Do you know who you are? Do you know whose you are? Do not be ashamed. Let's focus and grow together! We are on a mission to live in purpose and on purpose each and every day of our lives!

This book is for everyone and anyone who struggles with who they are, are struggling with life, and/or are struggling with their present with no hope for their future because they are stuck on their past.

My Daunting Childhood

Nonetheless, I can definitely say I have had a share of pain and hurt in my lifetime. But how do we heal from the pain? How do you find peace? Allow me to share painful events that have occurred in my life.

People think they know me, but they really don't. This is my story, my truth, my life. Here goes…

My childhood was all over the place. I did not have a normal childhood. I am the only girl of five children, and I am the oldest. Growing up, I witnessed domestic violence in the home. In the fifth grade, my life dramatically changed. My siblings and I were separated, and I never had a stable home after that. I was like a foster child within my family, going from one family member to another. Sometimes I did not know where I would live. I was not allowed to be a child anymore. I was not allowed to make any mistakes because if I did, I would not be able to live with that family anymore and would be sent to live with someone else. I was physically abused and neglected as a child. And I always felt like an outsider. I was taken advantage of and molested at the age of twelve, and I never saw my body the same again. I began to fight a lot, but that was my way of releasing my pain onto someone else.

As a child, I felt as if the odds were against me. I would hear my family speak so negatively about me. Sometimes, I would tell myself, *What is the use? Why try?* Many nights, I cried myself to sleep. But I knew I wanted more for myself even if they couldn't see it. I was determined to prove them wrong.

However, I always knew getting my education was the only thing that was going to set me free. I even tried to commit suicide when I thought that I had messed up my life and was not going to be able to graduate from high school. Since I had a teacher who believed in me, Ms. Jackson, and my counselor, Mrs. Myles, who helped me, I was able to graduate high school a year early and go off to college. College was my safe haven; it was my first place of stable living since fifth grade. Graduating from high school and going to college saved my life. Unfortunately, my hometown is where I am from and grew up, but it was never my home.

In the fifth grade, my brothers and I were separated. My brothers lived with our dad. I lived with another family member. This damaged our sibling bond. Our home living was not the best, but at least we had each other. I was no longer treated as an older sibling but as an only child who had to grow up fast. My body began to change and go through puberty. I had my first period, and I never received the proper guidance on how to take care of my body properly. I had many accidents until I figured out what to do to prevent them.

I went from a stable dysfunctional home to dysfunctional living. I stayed with one family member to the next. I wish I was protected as a little girl and that I was seen and loved. I was treated and felt like a burden. At the age of twelve, my innocence was taken from me. I was raped by someone I did not know. I had to stay at a family friend's house. The next day, I went to Dallas. Before I continue with that event, allow me to provide a side note. I have always loved car rides, looking out the window and looking at the scenery. I never went to sleep because I did not want to miss anything.

Okay, back to the previous event. On the way to Dallas, I went to sleep. I could not keep my eyes open for the life of me. When we made it to Dallas, I was left alone. I was still tired even though I slept the entire ride, which was about five to six hours. I tried to cook something to eat because I was hungry and did not eat anything all day. I boiled a hot dog, but unfortunately, I fell asleep. When I woke up, there was smoke everywhere, and a family friend told me to get up and go outside. I fell asleep while the hot dog was boiling.

Not one time did anyone ask me what happened. Why are you so tired? I wanted someone to be concerned about me, but no one cared. They cleaned the mess, and that was it. I tried to tell an older cousin, but she did not care. She just said I had sex. I never tried to tell anyone else. I did not speak about it again until I was an adult.

After being raped, I was not the same anymore. I didn't know how to tell anyone, but then again, I didn't think anyone cared. I was putting myself in bad situations. I struggled with saying no because I was scared that I would be taken advantage of anyway. When I would say no, I wasn't taken seriously. It was the grace of God that I didn't spiral out as a child and a young adult. I could have gotten pregnant at a young age but God. I could have gotten hooked on drugs and alcohol but God. Heck, I could have lost my mind but God.

Many times, as a child, I felt unloved and unwanted. I was forced to visit a relative that I did not feel comfortable around. He was verbally and physically abusive. When I was seven, I had to visit him one summer. He would get mad if I did not smile all the time, and he would say negative things to me. When I stayed with him, I had to take showers. I never took showers before, just baths. So one time, I slipped and fell, and my hair got wet and messed up. When I got out of the shower, I tried to tell him what happened, but he got so angry. He told me I did it on purpose. He told me to go to the couch and bend over. He covered my head with a pillow, and he beat me with his hand until I fell to the floor screaming. I cried every day until I went back home. I was so happy to tell my daddy, but I was too scared to tell him what happened. I remember hugging my daddy tightly and telling him I was glad to be back home.

On another occasion, I had to visit that relative. He beat me again because I did not speak to him properly. This time he did this at another relative's home. I remember my cousin watching me getting beaten. She didn't get help. She didn't say anything. At that moment, I felt like my life was hopeless.

The last incident occurred when I was thirteen years old. The relative came to visit, and he wanted me to spend time with him. I said no because I knew he would beat me. Unfortunately, I was forced to spend time with him. This time I tried to be smart and asked if my cousin could come, thinking that would prevent the beating. However, I just prolonged the beating. When we were returning home, I thought to myself, *Yes, nothing happened, and I was able to return safely.* But little did I know that we were just dropping my cousin off. I told him I was tired and wanted to go to bed. He told me I did not have a choice and forced me back into the car. I cried the entire ride. When he stopped the car, I jumped out of the car and ran screaming for help. He grabbed me, forced me back into the car, and beat me with his fist. He was hitting me in the face, and I tried my best to cover my face. Eventually, he stopped hitting me and drove me back to my uncle's house. I lay in bed and cried myself to sleep.

The next day, I went to my friend's house, and she saw the bruises on my face. I told her what happened, and she told her mom who told my family. When the relative came to visit that day, my family was standing outside. I remember one of my uncles confronting him about my bruises. He told him he better not touch me again. That uncle was as big as a toothpick, but his bark was as big as a pit bull. You did not want to mess with him. I appreciated him for standing up for me. Even though the relative still attempted to come around me again. He came up to my school as we were getting out of school for the day. I spotted his car and told my cousin we needed to run home as fast as we could. I never ran so fast in my life. We ran home avoiding the streets as possible, jumping fences and ducking in and out of areas until we made it to my uncle's house. My aunt let us in the house. We told her what was going on, and she hid me in the closet. I was so scared and believed if he beat me again, he would try to kill me.

At the beginning of my sophomore year in high school, I received a phone call stating that the relative was in prison. I thought that was the best news ever. I knew he did not go to prison for hurting me, but I knew his bad ways had caught up to him.

Please do not read this and feel sorry for me. Yes, that little girl went through some unimaginable things. And so many times, she thought her life was over. And she questioned, "God, why me? Why do I have to experience so much pain and hurt?" I didn't understand.

As I share this story, I can say I was beaten, but it didn't kill me. I was raped, but it didn't kill me. The memories cause feelings of pain and hurt, but I don't allow them to stop me from living. God has been with me every step of the way. I could have lost my life, but God kept me. I have a voice now. I will not be silenced. I will not be afraid. Someone needs to know that it is going to be okay. The feeling of pain or hurt may not totally disappear, but you learn to live with it, and that's a part of healing.

I am who I am because of what I been through. Now, do I wish my childhood or life experiences on anyone else? I definitely do not. No matter what I have been through, I love my family. Is everything perfect? No, it is not. But family is all you have. Don't hold on to the past. Create new memories, good memories, and live your life. Family drama is undeniable. Families fight. Families laugh and know how to have fun.

When people hear my name, they tell me it is beautiful and unique. My family named me, specifically my aunt Niecee and cousin Regina. My aunt gave me my first name, Kerriel. When I was little, I would tell people to think about the shampoo L'Oréal or the mermaid Ariel when trying to pronounce my name. My cousin gave me my middle name, Vontrise. When I found out how I truly got the name, I told myself that I was going to drop my middle name once I was married. Now, I will forever cherish my name. My cousin Regina died in a car accident. It was such a tragedy to my family. She was the diva of the family. And now she will forever live and have a special part of my life.

Create Your Own Family

In high school, I realized family is more than just the family you are born into. It is also people who love and support you and are there for you. There is the family you are born into, the family you create, and relatives who are just blood related.

Throughout my high school years, I lived with my cousin. She had her own family to take care of, and she wasn't that much older than me. She opened her home up to me, and I was very grateful.

In high school, I also lived with my two best friends at the time. Their parents opened their home to me and treated me like their own. If that's not family, then I don't know what is. They were loving and supportive. They saw the positive in me.

Growing up, you usually look up to an adult as a role model, but I looked up to my cousins as my role models, the good and the bad. My uncle Slim was my first role model and best friend. When he passed away when I was fifteen years old, my cousin/brother told me he got me. He stepped up and was really there for me. We had our moments too because we literally fought like siblings. My older cousin/sister was also there for me. She always let me hang out with her and her friends and made me feel included. Even with my role models, I still figured out my uniqueness because I always wanted to be my own person.

I love what I do, but I love who I am, and that's being a mom first. Harmony made me a mom biologically, but my godson made me a mom with the love we share. For the longest time, I would tell myself that I did not need to have any children and that my godson was enough. I was able to get and see him anytime I wanted to for the most part. I loved buying him things. Anything he asked for, I would find a way to get it. But the best part of it is that I was able to return him to his mom and live my life freely.

I always told myself that I did not want to bring a child into this world. This world is evil, and children should not have to suffer. Everyone around me was having children, but not me, and I was okay with that. There was so much I wanted to do and accomplish. Unfortunately, having a child was not in my plans. I also understood the responsibility of having a child, and my life at that time was not ready.

While I was an undergrad, my boyfriend at the time asked me would I have his baby. I told him, "Yes, but not right now." I guess he could not wait for me. We broke up, and he went and had a baby with someone else. I was crushed, but I got over it.

When I graduated from USM, I immediately moved to Nashville, Tennessee, to focus on my career. I remember when I was apartment searching, my brother/cousin was with me. He is biologically my cousin, but we grew up close like brothers and sisters. So I prefer to call him as my brother. But as we were looking at apartments, the leasing agent was asking about my preference for the apartment I was looking for. The first thing I said was that I would like more of a condo apartment with no one above me because I do not want to hear any children. I continued to say, "I work with children, so I would like to come home to a peaceful and quiet home." My brother looked at me and shook his head. At this time, he had two children that I love dearly, but I was serious about my quiet space.

Another instance occurred when my job was transferred to Memphis, Tennessee. I dated a guy, and he tried to make me have a baby for him. I ended things with him abruptly. Somehow, I immediately was in another relationship. This guy was not wanting me to have his baby because he already had two children. The children did not live with him, but when they came around, I was very uncomfortable. I still was not ready to be a mom, and I especially was not ready to be a stepmom. So I was glad when that relationship ended.

Then all of a sudden, while I was in the military, I was having a discussion with God. I told God I was ready to have a family and that I wanted the opportunity to be able to stay home with my child for the first year of his or her life. I understood the importance of the first year of a child's life especially being a psychology major and knowing the milestones that occur during that time. Once I had that conversation with God, I was comfortable with the thought of being a mom.

Not too long after my conversation with God, I got out of the military and moved to Houston, Texas, to live with my boyfriend. After a couple of months of living together, my boyfriend mentioned that he was surprised that I was not pregnant yet. Even though we had not discussed having a baby, neither one of us had a child. But I did know why I was not pregnant. Right before I got out of the military, I removed my birth control implant, but it was still affecting my body. So when my boyfriend mentioned pregnancy, I asked my doctor what helps with getting pregnant when you get off birth control. The doctor informed me prenatal vitamins help regulate your hormones and could help with pregnancy.

On my twenty-ninth birthday in 2015, I found out I was pregnant. I could not believe it. I had taken two pregnancy tests to make sure. I immediately made a doctor's appointment to confirm my pregnancy. It was happening. I was becoming a mom. I was scared and excited at the same time.

I always wanted to be a boy's mom, so when the doctor said we were having a girl, I could not believe it. I told myself, *What was I going to do with a girl?* All I knew was how to take care of boys. I am the only girl of four brothers. I grew up as a tomboy. I did not play with dolls or watch girlie shows. I did become more girlie in middle school, but I still liked to have fun with the boys. Then I loved helping with my godson. So again, what was I going to do with a girl?

All my life, I had always been tough and not affectionate enough. Was God giving me a girl to soften me up? But then it clicked in my head: God was giving me a girl so I could have the mother and daughter relationship I never had. I cried because God was giving me what I needed and not what I wanted.

So as everything was sinking in that I was becoming a mom, I began to prepare for my daughter. We bought a house that she could call home. The nursery was set up with everything she needed and more. I had two baby showers—one at work and one with family. I was definitely blessed to receive so many gifts that it was overwhelming to put everything in its place. But I was grateful that so many people were showering her with love.

However, my pregnancy was not the easiest. At the beginning of my pregnancy, I had vaginal bleeding. I went to the ER, and the doctor told me I was showing signs of a miscarriage. Oh, I was so scared because I did not want to lose my baby. I prayed and asked God to take care of my baby.

After I went through the miscarriage scare, I was sick a lot. I was either nauseous or vomiting because I could not keep food down. I experienced sickness in my first two trimesters. In my last trimester, it did not get better. I was not sick anymore, but I was so uncomfortable. My feet were full of fluid. I continued to work out until I could not work out anymore. So my pregnancy experience went from scary to miserable, and I was just ready for her to come.

I remember the countdown like it was yesterday. I went to the doctor for my thirty-seven-week checkup. I asked the doctor if it was safe for my baby to come. The doctor broke my strip and said that would help me dilate. A couple of hours later, I was at home taking a nap on the couch. I immediately got up and went to the bathroom. I was bleeding, and I told my daughter's father that it's time to go to the hospital.

I made it to the hospital; at first, the nurse said I was not dilated enough. I told them to contact my doctor because I was determined to have my baby. A few hours later, I was being sent to labor and delivery to prepare for the delivery of my baby. Wednesday, June 22nd of 2016, around 7:00 a.m., my baby girl entered the world, and my life was forever changed.

Many people do not know this, but the brain is not fully developed until the age of twenty-five. And I honestly believe people should not have a child until they are twenty-five years old. This would prevent children from having children. I truly believe that if this was the case, many children would not have to be a victim of abuse or neglect or even be killed. It takes a lot to be a parent, and even with support, sometimes, it is not enough. You must be mentally and emotionally capable to take care of a child.

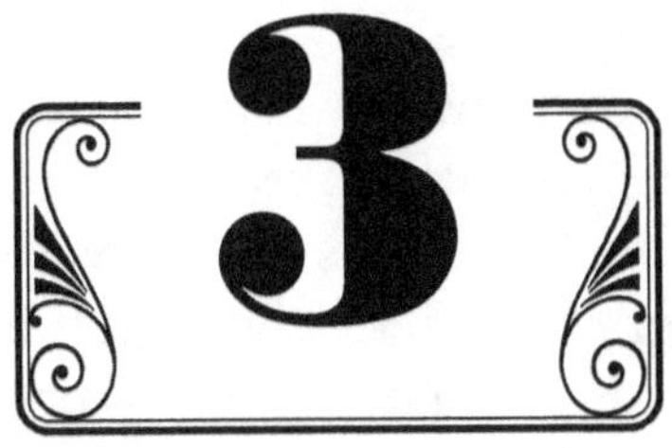

Learning to Cope with Grief throughout Life

When I was fifteen, I lost my first best friend, my uncle Leon "Slim." He was killed, and it broke my heart. He was ten years older than me. He always looked out for me. I lived with him back and forth when I lived in Dallas. I was back living in Mississippi for my high school years. I was at school when I found out about his death. I remember I fainted right on the school grounds. I could not believe my ears. I could not believe my best friend was gone. He was twenty-five years old when he died. And his death taught me that life is short and how I want to be remembered. And from that day forward, I started looking at life differently. I started taking my life more seriously. I knew I wanted to make something out of my life, and I understood that the next day was not promised.

In remembrance of my uncle Slim, I named my daughter after him. His name was Leon, and her middle name is Leona. I know he would have spoiled her rotten. My uncle Slim was small, but he was tough. He had heart, and he stood up for what he believed. He never backed down from a fight, literally. I do not know if that was the youngest child syndrome, but I admired his strength.

It has been over fourteen years since the passing of my grandmother. Oh, how I miss her every day. Many people say with time, grief gets better, but that is not wholeheartedly true. With time, you learn how to cope with them not being present, but it does not get better. I still to this day grieve my grandmother. I crave her cuddles and playing and doing my hair. I miss her stories and how she interacted with movies and TV shows.

During spring break of 2021, some of my family and I visited other family members in Austin, Texas. I got to see my cousins, whom I had not seen in a long time. But I was so happy to see my grandmother's baby sister, my great-aunt Pat. I had not seen her since my baby shower, which was in May 2016. When I saw her, so many emotions came over me. I was happy to see her because I could not believe how much she looked like my grandmother. On the other hand, I was sad because I wish she was actually my grandmother. I hugged her and said, "Aunt Pat, why do you look so much like my grandmother?"

My aunt Pat said, "She was my sister."

And we both laughed.

The entire time I was in her presence, I just hugged her. We had great conversations, and she shared some things with me that my grandmother spoke to her about.

I saw my aunt Pat another time that same year, but this time, it was not for a glorious occasion. My aunt Pat's brother, Uncle Earl "BaeBra" Martin, passed away, so we were attending his homegoing. As the family came together, we took pictures and created positive memories. And again, every time I was in her presence, I hugged her, not knowing that would be my last.

In August of that same year, 2021, my aunt Pat passed away from COVID-19. I cried so much! I was crying because of her death. I was also crying because it was like losing my grandmother all over again. The pain hurts so much. But I know they are in heaven with each other having a good ole time.

Unforgiveness Is a Burden

Are you holding on to the past? Have you forgiven others, but not forgiven yourself? Breathe, let go, be free, and set yourself free. In 2013, I was a part of a group called Ashes to Beauty. In the group, many things were shared that focused on the healing process. But it was in that group that I realized that I had not written a poem since my grandmother's death. My grandmother passed away in October 2008. And at that moment, I realized I was mad at God. I was mad that she was gone and I did not have more time with her. More than anything, I was mad at myself.

I lived with many family members throughout my childhood. Unfortunately, I did not have a stable living. Many times, I felt like a burden. I had to grow up fast. I could not enjoy being a child anymore. Anytime, I made a mistake, I was given to others like an unwanted package. I grew up with so much hurt and unforgiveness in my heart that it made me miss out on creating memories with others, positive memories.

In 2006 or 2007, the Martin family had our first family reunion that I knew of. I was living in Hattiesburg, Mississippi, attending the University of Southern Mississippi (USM). I was also working in my field as a clinical assistant working with homeless women and children. At the time of the family reunion, I was actually scheduled to be off, but I requested to be placed on the schedule. I did not want to attend the family reunion because there were family members I did not want to be around. But that decision caused me memories that I could have shared with my grandmother. That guilt and unforgiveness followed me for years after the death of my grandmother.

In 2019, my daughter and I lived in Atlanta for about seven months. During that time, we attended church and participated in activities. One Sunday morning, my eyes could not believe what I was seeing. There was a woman at the church who resembled my grandmother. She looked so much like my grandmother that I had to take a double look at her. At the church service, I sat near the woman and just stared at her. So after church service, I could not help myself. I went to the woman and introduced myself. I apologized for the impromptu conversation. I shared with the woman about my grandmother and how she looked so much like her. And the woman said, "Well maybe your grandmother is sending you a message." I knew at that moment what that message was. My grandmother was letting me know that all is well and everything is going to be okay. And when I felt that, I forgave myself.

But there was a point in my life when I made a mistake, and I thought my life was over. In my last year in high school, I was a junior the first semester and a senior the second semester. I had enough credits to graduate early, and I knew that was the best route for me. At the end of the first semester, I got into an argument with a classmate. The classmate was bigger than me, so I knew I had to defend myself. I carried a blade in my purse for protection. I pulled the blade out of my purse and held it in my hand. I did not think the classmate knew I had a blade. The classmate was sent to the office because she was known for causing a disturbance in the classroom. I stayed in the classroom and calmed down, dismissing the argument.

The next morning at school, the officer came into my first-period class and told me to follow him with my purse. My heart started beating fast. I walked into the office with the officer, and the principal was waiting. I gave the officer my purse, and he began to search through it. I knew what he was looking for, but I was hoping he did not find it. That was not the case. He found the blade, and tears began to roll down my face. There was nothing I could say or do because I was found guilty at that moment.

The police officer took me to the police station. Luckily, I did not have to wear handcuffs or ride in the back of the police car, but it was still embarrassing, leaving campus with the police officer. When we made it to the police station, I lost it. I began to cry uncontrollably. I felt like a criminal because I had to do fingerprints and take mugshots. It was the worst day of my life.

When my grandmother came, I saw the disappointment on her face, and that broke my heart even more. I was living with my cousin at the time, so my grandmother took me to her home. I went into my room and locked the door and began to cry and scream and cry and scream. My cousin lived on the second floor, so I told myself I did not want to live anymore and that my life was over because I was not going to be able to graduate. I banged my head on the wall, telling myself I was so stupid. I had a huge knot on my forehead. My head was pounding in pain. I let the window up in my room. As I was getting ready to jump, my cousin pushed the door open to my room. I do not know if I would have died that day, but I was willing to find out.

I was expelled from my high school. I was not allowed on campus without an adult. I had to go in front of the school board and superintendent. Due to not having any prior behavior incidents and being an honor student, I was able to attend the alternative school the second semester. The school was for students with behavior issues, so I felt out of place. I cried my first week because I felt like a criminal. The students had to go through a metal detector every day. But I showed no weakness and just focused on my schoolwork so I could graduate. I received my work from the high school weekly. I met with the guidance counselor regularly to complete my English 4 course with Mississippi State. I was not able to participate in any senior activities. But I was still able to graduate and attend graduation, and that's all that mattered to me.

That incident was a successful regret. That mistake almost cost my life, but God brought an amazing person in my life, Ms. Jackson, who healed me, gave me hope, and guided me in the right direction for success in my future.

Previous mistakes in my life just involved me, but this mistake not only involved me but my daughter as well. I knew God had forgiven me, but I struggled with forgiving myself. I was so hard on myself. How could I go out of order? I lived with someone without being married. I got pregnant and had a child. I thought my life was all together, but I was living a worldly fairytale. In my eyes, my life was such a disappointment. Now I am a single mom. I cried and I cried. I asked the Lord to not let my daughter suffer because of my mistakes and wrongdoings. I never wanted this life for my daughter. I wanted to give her what I never had, a stable two-parent home.

But then I remembered when I prayed to God and said I was ready to have a family. God never told me what my family would look like. I was not specific in my prayer. It all began to make sense to me. God already knew how things were going to turn out. My daughter and I are a family. It may not look like how I may have wanted it to be, but I have accepted it. I know my daughter and I are not alone. It's me, my daughter, and God, and I know with that combination, we are going to be alright.

It took me a while to forgive and live, but when I did, I felt the weight of my shoulders being free. See you cannot blame your family for how your life become. You have the choice to do better and live better. When you know better, you do better.

Education Was My Freedom

I have always taken my education seriously. I graduated high school a year early. I graduated undergraduate a semester early. I went and got my masters in mental health counseling, and I got my doctorate in psychology. My grandma once told me, "They can take away your career, your house, your job, but they cannot take away your education," and that's how I knew knowledge is power. I have always been a self-determined, motivated, hardworking individual. I strive to do and be my best in all that I do.

Education has always been my go-to. It was like my get-out-of-jail-free card/distraction from what was really going on in my life. From middle school to high school, I did not have a stable life. But I knew if I graduated high school and went to college, I would live in a dorm, and that would be my place of living.

In undergrad, my freshman year, my dad got into a bad wreck while working. Registration sent me a bill of a hundred and something dollars that I owed. I did not have the money, and I did not want to bother my dad because of his situation. I did not have anyone at the time to assist me.

I ended up getting two jobs, one as a server and the other one at a fast-food restaurant, while taking twenty-one hours that semester. I was so overwhelmed, but I knew getting my education would help me get a better career so I could financially support myself.

I started my master's program in September 2008, and my grandmother passed away in October of that same year. I was devastated, and I tried to quit school. But I had a professor who was caring and understanding. She helped me through that class, and then and therefore, I gave all my energy to my education.

So many changes occurred while I was getting my doctorate. I began the program in January 2016 while pregnant with my daughter. I had my daughter in June 2016. I stopped working and became a stay-at-home mom. That year for my thirtieth birthday, my daughter's father bought me my dream car, a Mercedes. In May 2017, I got engaged. I returned to the work field in August 2017. March 2018, we called the wedding off. In August 2018, we ended our relationship. In December 2018, my daughter and I moved to Atlanta. In August 2019, we moved back to Houston. We went through a child support custody battle from August 2019 to October 2020.

In March 2020, the coronavirus pandemic impacted the world. In May 2020, George Floyd was murdered by a police officer, and his death impacted the United States. In June 2020, I experienced racism and pushback from my chair. A complaint was filed and resolved. I received a new chair in July 2020 who told me that I was not going to graduate, and he does not even know how I made it this far in the program. I was distraught at this point. In August 2020, I attempted to drop the doctoral program and just receive another master's degree. Fortunately, financial aid informed me that I had to complete my current class and could not enroll in another class. I filed another complaint. My chair was changed again for the second time. But God.

In September 2020, I received a new chair. Hopefully, my third and last one. This chair came in like a superhero. He said, "I do not understand the problem of why you are not finished, but the goal is to have you finish in the next couple of months." His optimism gave me my mojo again. We worked great together. All deadlines were met. December 2020, I defended my dissertation. February 2021, the dean approved my dissertation. October 2021, I attended my graduation ceremony.

I say all this to say I went through many obstacles while getting my doctorate. I could have given up. Heck, I tried to stop the program. But God! He had a plan for my life. So when my fiancé and I ended in 2018, I threw all my energy into finishing my doctoral program. I knew it was my responsibility to give my daughter the life she deserved.

Getting my doctorate was the hardest thing I ever did in my life. Life does not stop just because you are getting your doctorate. I began the program in 2016, and I was also pregnant with my daughter at the time. When I first started, I told myself, *I can do this*. Then it became too much. I took many breaks throughout the program. While getting my doctorate, I worked until I had my baby, and then I became a stay-at-home mom. I completed my first residency in the summer of 2017 and met my friend/colleague Dr. Demira. When my daughter turned one, I went back into the work field. I worked two jobs, went to school, was a mom, and was engaged to be married at the time.

In 2018, I attended my second residency. But my life changed drastically when my wedding was called off two months before we were supposed to get married. At the end of 2018, my daughter and I moved to Atlanta. We stayed in Atlanta for seven months and then moved back to Houston. I defended my prospectus in May of 2019. I defended my proposal in December 2019. I completed my research and conducted my interviews, but the process continued to get harder.

The closer I was getting to the end of my doctoral program, the harder it was becoming. I began to experience racism and discrimination. At one point, I wanted to give up. I tried to give up and just accept getting another master's degree and not finish the doctoral program. But God had other plans for me. I went through three chairs on my committee as I was completing the program. On December 9, 2020, I defended my dissertation and became Dr. Lyles. In February 2021, my dissertation was approved by the dean. However, due to COVID, I was not able to attend my graduation ceremony until October 2021, but it was worth the wait.

My dissertation will forever be dear to my heart. The title of my dissertation was "Black Middle-Class Women Describe Their Experiences That Influenced Their Decisions to be Stay-at-Home Mothers." I chose to write about the topic because I was that mother and there was not much research supporting the topic.

Here are findings and recommendations that I hope will enlighten you about my dissertation topic and encourage you to share with other mothers.

This qualitative descriptive study's goal was to provide a comprehensive summarization of specific events experienced by Black middle-class stay-at-home mothers (Lambert & Lambert 2012). Furthermore, this study provided a platform for Black middle-class women to share their personal experiences that influenced their decisions to be stay-at-home mothers.

Due to the history of slavery and the legacy of institutional discrimination, Black mothers have a deep history and high prevalence of participation in the paid labor force (Curenton, Crowley, and Mouson 2018).

Even though society has placed such negative social stereotypes on single Black mothers, higher-income mothers have a sense of accomplishment and confidence as they endure being single Black mothers (Mandara, Johnston, Murray, and Varner 2008). In my study, the participants acknowledged their accomplishments as being a Black middle-class woman in a world focused on social class, gender, and race.

Throughout the history of welfare and childcare, implicit messages have always implied that Caucasian mothers stay at home with their children, while Black mothers go to work (Dow 2016). In my study, many participants implied that many Black middle-class moms worked, but they wanted more for their family despite the color of their skin.

Black mothers may not fit into the norms of society, but they are forceful women who demand respect and attention as motherhood is an achievement of power (Odum 2017). In my study, the participants described their kids as an investment and the importance of valuing their own dreams and goals.

Hayden (2017) identified many myths that shaped the public's perception of Black motherhood such as the mammy that emerged from slavery; the faithful, obedient domestic servant caring for the Caucasian family better than her own; and the welfare queen depending on the public dime. In my study, the participants made it known that they wanted to break the stereotype of a Black woman.

Educated Black women are expected to focus on their careers, so it was routine for a Black mother to return to work (Giele 2008). In my study, many of the participants stated that during early adulthood, they wanted to set themselves up for success and to do their best.

Educated Black families make better parenting decisions than non-educated families (Riina and McHale 2012). In my study, the participants stated that their education did not influence them, but it allowed them the opportunity to be stay-at-home moms.

Family and community expectations have made Black mothers feel compelled to work despite their desire to prioritize raising their children (Dow 2016). In my study, the participants acknowledged that their careers did not influence them to be stay-at-home mothers but provided them the opportunity to be stay-at-home moms.

For some women who have always worked, motherhood shifts in identity and responsibilities cause a woman to become financially dependent on her spouse for the first time (Anderson, Webster, and Barr 2018). In my study, the participants discussed being mindful about spending money and being able to partake in extracurricular activities.

On average, Black women receive significantly lower earnings than white men and women but work longer hours, which decreases their investment in their children, impacting their social and cognitive development and their overall success (Patterson 2017). In my study, the participants stated how they want to make sure their family is comfortable and set up for success.

Historically, Black women are viewed as laborers, and working after birth was a normal part of motherhood (Lu, Wang, Han, and Wang 2017). In my study, many of the participants described their childhoods and family backgrounds regarding the mother working to provide and the lack of presence in their lives.

While Caucasian mothers who stay at home receive public approval for their actions, Black mothers are subject to more negative scrutiny due to traditionally having to work for pay (Curenton, Crowley, and Mouzon 2018). In my study, the participants discussed wanting more for their families and not allowing society to impact their decisions.

The practical implications of this study imply that Black mothers are only laborers, Black-middle class mothers are overlooked, and negative images of Black mothers not spending parenting time with their children.

The most important strategy that was provided in this research was breaking the generational curse of cultural influence.

Society must provide equal opportunities to all mothers and ensure family-friendly employment that can provide mothers with a substantial amount of maternal leave and flexibility that mothers to be involved parents.

Work-life balance is an essential factor in allowing women to work effectively and provide their motherly duties.

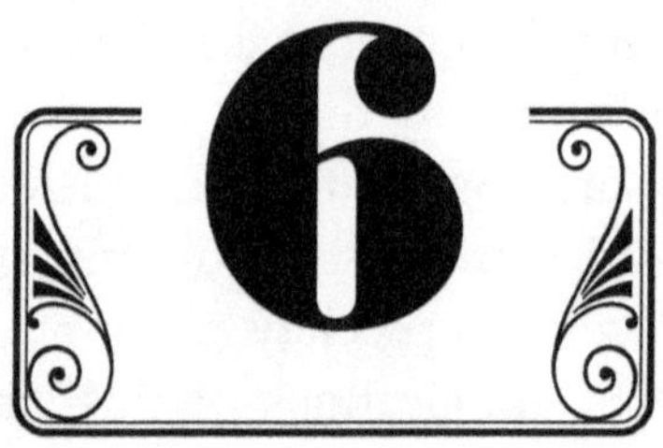

Awaiting My One True Love

Sometimes, I look over my life, and I ask myself, *Was I too focused on my education that I did not allow love to find me?*

Now, do not get me wrong. I had a high school sweetheart, but it was so much drama with the relationship that my education was still at the forefront. I got hurt like any typical girl in a relationship. And we stayed together up until the end of my freshman year in college.

After that relationship ended, I immediately was in another relationship. Honestly, I thought this guy was going to be my husband. We would ride to campus together. We would stay nights at each other's place. He spoiled me, and he was there when I needed him. We even had a dog together; she was like our baby. When there were no more of us, my heart was broken. He was my first true love. So I wanted to graduate and just leave, and that's what I did.

After him, my heart was not the same. I built a wall, kept my guard up, and did not allow myself to be too vulnerable. I will never forget that right before I graduated, there was this guy whom I worked with that really liked me. We talked for a short moment. But he asked me to stay in Hattiesburg after graduation so we could be together. He wanted to make me his wife and build me a house. I thought he was out of his mind. I was only twenty years old at the time, so I never talked to him again.

I would talk to guys but would abruptly stop talking to them when they wanted to get serious. I knew I was not ready for that emotionally or mentally. So did I miss out on opportunities for love?

Years later, around 2010, I moved from Nashville to Memphis, Tennessee. I ended up in a relationship. Right before graduating from graduate school, I had to take a comprehensive exam to graduate. I failed the exam the first time. I blamed it on the relationship because I felt like it was too much drama and stress. I stayed in the relationship but shifted my energy more to me graduating, and I passed the exam a month later.

He attended my graduation with me, and a conversation sparked regarding where we see each other in the next three to five years. As I stated my future goals, I realized he was not included. I think I was with him for security, which is weird to say because he was very insecure and controlling.

After that relationship, I told myself that I needed to focus back on myself. I joined the military in August 2013. I was able to get away from all the chaos. I focused on myself and reconnected with God. In 2014, I was at my best friend's wedding. I reconnected with an ex who pursued me for six years. At this point in my life, I was truly ready to give love another try. It was like a fairytale. Everything that I wanted was happening. I had the man, the baby, the house, the car, and financial security. I allowed myself to love again. But then the fantasy ended, and reality almost took me out.

Having my daughter, I thought my life was complete. I had the family, a nice house, and my dream car. What else could a girl ask for? But my life changed drastically in a blink of an eye. As my wedding day approached, May 26, 2018, the wedding was called off exactly two months before. I thought I was living in a nightmare, and I just wanted to wake up, but everything was falling apart.

We tried professional counseling because we participated in two different premarital counseling sessions. We agreed to push the wedding date back further to give us time to work things out. But we were growing further apart. He moved out of our home on May 30, 2018. We continued therapy until August of 2018, and once that was over, we were over.

I was devastated. I was embarrassed. I was depressed. I felt all alone. I became a statistic, a single black mom. I never wanted to be seen as a "baby momma." I cried and I cried. At the time, I was working two jobs. I was teaching and subbing. I was in school, getting my doctorate. And now I had to add being a single mom on top of all of that. I did not know how I was going to do it. I could not believe this was my life.

As I cried one night, I asked the Lord to help me. I needed help with my situation because I did not know what to do. The Lord definitely works in mysterious ways. A couple of days later, one of my friends who lived in Atlanta randomly reached out to me. She said, "You and your family should move to Atlanta."

And I said to myself, *Where did this come from?* I messaged her back, "I might just do that, but it's just me and my baby."

She immediately messaged me back and said, "You guys are welcome to live with me for a while until you get on your feet."

I said, "Lord, I do not know what to make of this, but this may be a good idea."

Then I reached out to one of my Marine sisters who lived in Atlanta, but I had not talked to her since I got out of the military in 2015. I told her my situation, and just like that, she invited me and my daughter to live in her home because she was rarely there anyway. I was so excited. I said, "God, this is working out. Everything is coming together." I talked to my boss about teaching online. I found Harmony a school. We were moving during the Christmas break of 2018. The only person I had to share this information with that probably would not like it was my daughter's father.

So, of course, he did not like the idea of us moving, but he did not try to stop us either. We had an agreement that he would move back into the house while I was gone. I did not know how long I was going to live in Atlanta, but I knew I had to leave Houston for a while. I cried as I was leaving because the life I once had was truly over. And if and when I returned, my life would never be the same.

My daughter and I got to Atlanta and got situated. After a couple of days, my two-year-old daughter said, "I am ready to go home."

I told her, "This is our home for right now."

She said, "No, our own house."

And at that moment, tears began to fall from my eyes. I grabbed her, and I just held her tight in my arms. Then I began to question myself. Was I doing the right thing? Will we be okay? Will my daughter be okay? I asked God for strength and guidance because I definitely needed it.

We ended up living in Atlanta from the end of December 2018 to the end of July 2019. During that time, my daughter attended school, did gymnastics, and played soccer. I tried my best to keep her occupied, so she did not feel sad that we were not in our own home.

In a relationship, you devote so much that you lose yourself. I had to find myself again. I had lost myself in my relationship. I no longer knew who I was anymore. I focused on rekindling my relationship with God. I did not realize I put my relationship before God. I went before God and asked Him to forgive me. I fasted and prayed. I meditated and spent time with God. We attended church there. I was doing everything I needed to do to put my life back together. But it was not easy.

When life throws you a curve ball, it's hard putting yourself back out there. As I was healing, dating was the last thing on my mind. My friends and family would encourage me to get back out there. But I was not ready mentally or emotionally. It was like I was isolated in another world, and I could not focus on anything else until the goal had been accomplished. I know it's easy for me to say I am celibate or abstinent because I am not in a relationship or interacting with someone and waiting can be the hard part.

But I am not giving up on love. I know my Boaz is out there. I am a sucker for love. I love reading and watching love stories. I know and believe I will love again. The right man, the man God has for me, will come along, and I will be ready. Until then, I will dream and wait for my love. My love story is still in the making…

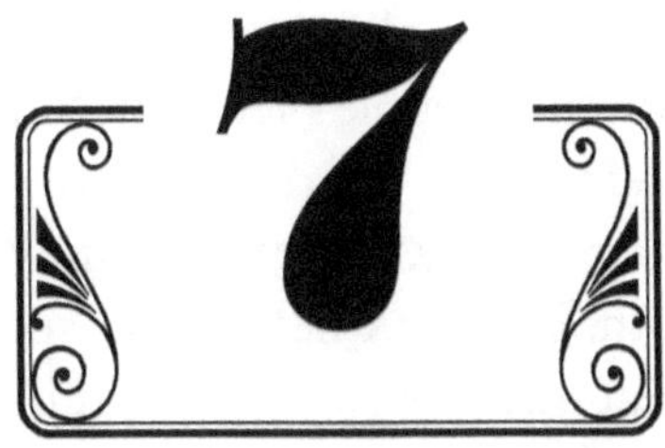

In Order to Heal, You Must Deal with the Hurt

Growing up, I felt like an outsider and that I did not fit in with my own family. I struggled with the way my body looked. I didn't want the attention my body portrayed. Many people would compliment me on my shape, but deep down inside, I hated the way I looked. The way older guys or creepy men would look at me would creep me out. I wanted to be smaller and not seen as the thick girl. I battled with eating disorders in high school up until my freshman year in college. Sometimes I would work out too much just to make sure I would see a difference in my weight. At one point, I had gotten so small that a family member told me that my face looked sucked in. I don't think I ever accepted my body shape fully, but I did come to grasp that I was causing more harm to myself than helping myself.

People do not realize the power of the tongue and how words can be so hurtful. The word *why* is such an offensive word. In the field of psychology, we are taught to never use the word *why* when talking with clients and patients. The saying goes, "If you do not have anything nice to say, do not say anything at all." Many people are so inconsiderate of other people's feelings. Saying things like, "Girl, you are skinny," or "Girl, you have gained weight," are not nice things to say. You never know what a person is struggling with. So think before you speak, and always remember to treat others how you would like to be treated.

To this day, I have a fear of being obese and dying of cancer. Many family relatives have died from these diseases. Gaining weight scares me. In my entire pregnancy, I worked out. I still gained fifty pounds, but the doctor stated that was mostly fluid. After my pregnancy and when I was cleared by the doctor to move around more, I immediately began working out to get back in shape to my pre-pregnancy weight.

I can definitely say the vegan lifestyle has helped me tremendously. I work out at least three times a week. Working out is my stress reliever, physically and mentally. But on the other hand, I believe this lifestyle can help me prevent and/or prolong cancer. Cancer is prevalent on both sides of my family. It really scared me. Since 2018, there have been five deaths in my family from cancer alone. To say the least, the fear is there, but I am doing my best to take care of my health and live a healthy lifestyle.

I have not eaten meat since 2017. I am vegan, and I am not just you know eat vegan, but I live a vegan lifestyle. It is for health and for lifestyle purposes that are beneficial for me and my daughter. We became vegan when my daughter was one year old. The only meat she has ever had was salmon and tuna. I struggle with IBS, and it is hard for my body to break down or digest meats and dairy products. While I was breastfeeding my daughter, she also struggled with constipation. Not only that, but my daughter is also allergic to dairy. I educate my daughter on the importance of eating healthy and where meat and dairy products come from. She loves animals and does not want to hurt them, and she states that's why she wants to be a veterinarian.

Then I deflected my behaviors to becoming a shopaholic. I would go shopping when I felt sad, mad, or happy. I always found a reason to shop. I had more credit cards than I could keep up with. When I graduated from college, I had accumulated so much debt. I knew I needed to change my spending habits. For the new year of 2009, the pastor at the church declared all members to become debt-free. Shredders were provided at church. I brought all my credit cards to the altar and shredded each one of them. I told myself that I would not get another credit card until I was more responsible. If I didn't have the money to purchase something, then it meant that I did not need it. I realized that I was not dealing with my problems in a healthy manner. I was going from one unhealthy behavior to another. But enough was enough. I looked my problems in the face and said it was time to heal and stop causing unnecessary problems in my life.

I did not realize until I was older that I had mommy issues. I knew I never had a really good relationship with my mom, and I always felt like a motherless child. It was when I got older and was trying to understand myself and my life that I realized that I had mommy issues. Unfortunately, it just did not start with me; it was from generations before me as well.

For most of my life, I feel like I was proving to my family that I was enough. I always felt like an outsider. Family does not realize the expectations that they put on family members and how their words impact others. I was born with curses and generational cycles in my life. Many people have daddy issues, but I had mommy issues. And I was not the first in my family to have those issues.

All my childhood life, I was proving myself to others; it took me a long time to start living for myself. That literally happened later in my life. For the majority of the first half of my life, I was living and proving myself to others that I was more than who they said I was going to be. I graduated high school a whole year early, and that still was not enough. I went to college, and it was still like they were waiting for me to mess up. It was not until I went to the military that I realized and told myself that I had to stop living for everyone else and live for myself. It was not about proving myself to others anymore but to live life freely.

Joining the US Marine Corps changed my life forever. I will always be grateful for being able to join the military because it helped me to accept myself and to live a life for myself. Many people usually joined the military right after high school, but I joined the military at a latter part of my life. I wanted to join when I got out of high school, but that didn't happen, so it was still in my heart to do so. I was twenty-six when I joined the military. I was getting burnt out from my field, and I needed a change in my life. I got into the field of psychology at the age of nineteen while I was still an undergrad. I was so passionate about what I do. I love the field of psychology, in helping others and serving others and being that support for others, but sometimes you can be so supportive of others and give your all to others that you forget about yourself.

Oh, how I loved my experience in the military, but I would never recommend anyone to go in at such a late age, except if you're going into the Air Force or Navy, you'll be alright. Okay, I am just playing my military brothers and sisters. But honestly joining the military at a late age definitely puts a toll on your body. My body is definitely suffering from things that I did in the military even years later. A Marine saying is, "You are not broke unless you are broken." Now I hate that saying.

I have nerve damage in my back. I have nerve damage in my right elbow to my fingers. I also have nerve damage in my right foot. This is just a few of the aches and pains my body has endured. You only have one body; take care of it. Know your body's limits.

Do not get me wrong; I enjoyed my experience in the military. I was meritoriously promoted in combat training. I received the Certificate of Commendation while serving as class leader and the selection for honor graduate at my MOS and received the best plaque ever from my station in the field. However, it had its share of racism and sexism as well. The military is a "man's world," and at times, you can feel out of place. But always stand your ground with your head held high.

Since I was forced to grow up so fast and was not able to express myself, as a young adult, I expressed myself in childish ways because I did not know any better. I would throw temper tantrums when I would not get my way.

I began getting tattoos in high school, and I saw it as a way of creating art on my body, putting reminders on my body to encourage myself. My tattoos are sacred and are only visible to others when I choose to display them.

My childhood traumatized me. I would get into relationships wanting people to love me because I did not get that from my own family or I did not feel loved. As I grew up and became an adult and went through therapy, I learned how to cope with my trauma. But the trauma never goes away you just learn how to cope with it. It still comes and has an impact on your decision-making and how you go about life. You learn how to deal with it, especially in a healthy way.

I am really thankful for USM because I utilized the resources that were provided to me. USM provided students with counseling for psychology majors. It was for extra credit, but I definitely took it seriously because I was going through some things, and I needed someone to talk to. It really helped me with a lot of things that I was going through like a breakup, family issues, and anxiety. That was my first time going to therapy.

Going to counseling is definitely a part of my growth. There's a saying in the field of psychology that to counsel someone else, you have to be counseled yourself. A person's mind is just as important as their physical. So just like when you get your physical exams annually, you should also get mental check-ins annually. It should be required in career organizations for their employees to do and get mental check-ins. So many people have dealt with trauma. And hurt people hurt people.

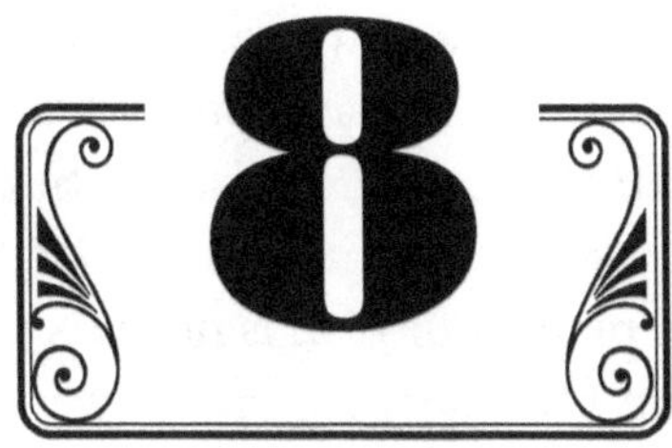

I Am Here because of Him

Everything will not be easy, but with the Lord on your side, anything is possible. I have always had a relationship with God, but as I got older, I understood what that really meant. Many people will say that they grew up in the church, but what does that really mean that you grew up in the church? Do you focus on religion, or do you have an actual relationship with God? Where would I be without God? Nowhere, I tell you. I remember that when I was a little girl, I walked to the front of the church and said, "I love the Lord, and I want to be baptized." I believe I was either seven or eight years old. Throughout my life, God has been with me. When I felt all alone, I knew God was with me. In middle school, when I would have to walk to school by myself at times for practice, I would pray that I make it to school safely. I know many times in my life, I could have been dead and gone or something really bad happening to me, but I knew God was with me. So yes, I grew up in the church, but I was not a bench rider, but I knew going to church fed me spiritually. So no matter what was going on in my life, I found a church to attend.

I also understood the power of prayer. Prayer changes things. He might not show up when I want Him, but He is always right on time. Fast and pray when you need to be reconnected with the Lord. He listens. Surrender it all to Him. It's not for you to figure it out. Your life may not be falling into your plan. Your plan is not His plan. Just talk to Him and wait on Him because He answers prayers.

In October 2008, when my grandmother was on her sick bed in the hospital, she kept singing to the Lord. Not one time did she say the Lord had forsaken her. She still glorified His name.

I have witnessed and experienced many things growing up. Because of that, I grew up fast. Now I am mindful of how things can affect you. I no longer play secular music. I realized that type of music was not uplifting and was not having a positive effect on my mental or emotions. I stopped drinking for two years because I wanted to make sure I was not allowing alcohol to hinder my decision-making. Now I occasionally drink red wine. It has health benefits, but I am not dependent upon it.

It has been years since I have cursed. I realized I did not have to curse to get my point across. And the respect I have for myself also shows others how to respect and communicate with me. Also, my childhood was full of drama and confrontation, so I make sure to not surround myself with negativity. Creating healthy boundaries are crucial to my well-being, so removing myself from negativity is not a problem. It's growth.

I understand we all do not get it right, and we all mess up. But God will never leave us or forsake us. Tomorrow is a new day. And if He gives us a new chance to get it right, we should ask Him for guidance and forgiveness, repent of our sins, and do our best to live in purpose and on purpose every day of our lives. Let your light shine even in the midst of darkness. And do not dare let anyone or anything dim your light. Do not be ashamed to live for the Lord, because you are either living for Him or living for the world. We were created to be in this world to make a difference and to use our gift to glorify His name.

The following are scriptures and songs that have blessed my life:

- Psalm 23: My daddy encouraged me to say this scripture when I was in college, and I have been saying it every day since. I actually said this scripture when I was in boot camp in the military. I could not swim, but I had to pass the swim test. I jumped off the ten-foot lever five times before I made it across. The last time, I said, "Lord, I cannot keep jumping off this lever. I need this to be the last time." So I closed my eyes, jumped off the lever, and started saying Psalm 23 to myself. When I opened my eyes, I swam across. That was nothing but God.

- Lecrae 8:28: This is one of my favorite songs. It literally says that it is all going to work out sooner than later and we do not have to worry about tomorrow. When I first listened to this song, I cried. I was so stressed out, and I felt like my life was in shackles. But this was also the time in my life that I transitioned from listening to secular music. I realized that we need to be careful with what we listen to and what we surround ourselves. I knew I was in a place in my life where I needed to be uplifted and encouraged. I needed songs that had meaning. So 2019 was the last time I played secular music.

Our memories make us who we are. Life is short, so creating positive memories is important. Memories are everlasting. Gifts and things come and go, but memories are always with us.

The following are sayings and scriptures that I say on a daily basis:

- Pray Until Something Happens—this is actually the name of my Bible study book club, which is shortened as PUSH.
- The Serenity Prayer—God, grant me the serenity to accept the things I cannot change, courage to change the things I can, and wisdom to know the difference—living one day at a time; enjoying one moment at a time; accepting hardship as the pathway to peace; taking, as Jesus did, this sinful world as it is, not as I would have it; trusting that He will make all things right if I surrender to His will, that I may be reasonably happy in this life and supremely happy with Him forever in the next. Amen.
- The Whole Armor of God—Put on all the armor that God gives you so that you will be able to stand up against the Devil's evil tricks. For we are not fighting against human beings but against the wicked spiritual forces in the heavenly world, the rulers, authorities, and cosmic powers of this dark age. So put on God's armor now! Then when the evil day comes, you will be able to resist the enemy's attacks; and after fighting to the end, you will still hold your ground. So stand ready, with truth as a belt tight around your waist, with righteousness as your breastplate, and as your shoes the readiness to announce the Good News

of peace. At all times, carry faith as a shield; for with it, you will be able to put out all the burning arrows shot by the evil one. And accept salvation as a helmet and the Word of God as the sword, which the spirit gives you.

Consider it pure joy, my brothers and sisters, whenever you face trials of many kinds, because you know that the testing of your faith produces perseverance. (James 1:2–3)

But if we hope for what we do not see, we wait for it with patience. (Romans 8:25)

I have told you these things, so that in me you may have peace. In this world you will have trouble. But take heart! I have overcome the world. (John 16:33)

But as for me, I will watch expectantly for the Lord, I will wait for the God of my Salvation. My God will hear me. (Micah 7:7)

Point your kids in the right direction when they're old they won't be lost. (Proverbs 22:6)

Yes indeed, it won't be long now, God's Decree. Things are going to happen so fast your head will swim, one thing fast on the heels of the other. You won't be able to keep up. Everything will be happening at once—and everywhere you look, blessings! (Amos 9:13–15)

For I know the plans I have for you, and the thoughts I think towards you. They are good and not evil; they will give you hope and expected end. (Jeremiah 29:11)

Trust in the Lord will all your heart and lean not on your own understanding; in all your ways submit to Him and He will make your paths straight. (Proverbs 3:5–6)

I can do all things through Christ who strengthens me. (Philippians 4:13)

At one point of my life, I could not stop crying. I was so tired of crying. And one of my spiritual leaders shared the following with me: Psalm 126:5–6, "Tears and Brokenness in Victorious Warfare, Faith's Warfare."

Tears in scripture play a unique role in spiritual breakthrough. Here we discover that the planting of seeds accompanied by a spirit of brokenness will not only bring a spiritual harvest of results but will leave the sower a spirit of rejoicing in the process. This passage, along with numerous others in the scripture regarding spirit of brokenness, pictures a variety of purposes and functions related to what might be termed "ministry of tears," a ministry Charles H. Spurgeon defined as liquid prayer. First, there are tears of sorrow or suffering (2 Kings 20:5). Second, there are tears of joy (Genesis 33:4). Third, there are tears of compassion (John 11:35). Fourth, there are tears of desperation (Esther

4:1, 3). Fifth, there are tears of travail, or giving birth (Isiah 42:14). Sixth, there are tears of repentance (Joel 2:12, 13). Passion is spiritual warfare which is clearly needed.

This passage gave me a better understanding of tears and their meaning throughout life situations.

Poems were an outlet for me to express my feelings. I used to love writing poems. I actually wrote a poem for my uncle Slim and read it at his funeral. When my grandmother passed, I wrote a poem for her funeral. It had been fourteen years since I wrote a poem for a funeral until the tragic passing of my cousin Regina.

A poem I wrote as I was overcoming brokenness:

> Who am I? I am beautiful. I am hard working. I am loving and my God loves me. Who am I? I am confident. I am fearless. I am forgiven for my God forgives me for all my sins. Who am I? I am smart. I am loyal. I am thankful that the Lord created such a unique person. Who am I? I am letting go of my past. I am accepting my present. I am looking forward to future endeavors for the Lord has many blessings for me. Who am I? I am a phenomenal woman; that's me.

AUTHOR'S NOTE

I have told you these things, so that in me you may have peace. In this world you will have trouble. But take heart! I have overcome the world.
—John 16:33 NIV

People will look at your accomplishments and say, "I want to be like you." But do they really? Do they really want to walk a mile in my shoes? Do they really understand what I had to go through? The tears that I had to cry? That depression and anxiety that I experienced? Be careful with your words because do you really want to be like me?

In life, you are going to lose yourself, but do not be ashamed of finding yourself. Take time out for yourself. Take time out to meditate, and take time out to do what's best for you. Find your true self, and always walk in your truth.

I share my testimony not because I want to but because I have to. I have to be obedient to God. A while ago, I asked God to use me to help me live the life He has for me and to serve His people to glorify and magnify His name. Then I understood my gift. I am a servant of the Lord who teaches and educates His people. To teach and educate others is the willingness to be open and transparent, to keep it real but respectful, to keep it real but humble, and to keep it real but loving.

The field of psychology has always intrigued me, the study of the mind and behavior, to learn and understand self and how we interact with others. When I entered the field of psychology, I was young. I was nineteen years old and had just completed my sophomore year in college. I was working with homeless women and children. I was a clinical assistant. I worked the night shift, 7:00 p.m. to 7:00 a.m. The shifts were like a nurse's schedule. I attended school during the day. I enjoyed the experience as it was a foot in the door to other opportunities in the field.

Preparing for graduation, I applied for positions in many different states. I wanted to get away from Mississippi and explore new experiences. My supervisor at the time suggested I work with teenagers. She felt that would be a good fit, given my stern personality and adaptability. I took her advice and moved to Nashville, Tennessee, where I began working with teens in need. I have been working with teens and young adults ever since.

> Listen to advice and accept instruction,
> that you may gain wisdom in the future.
> (Proverbs 19:20)

> Where there is no guidance, a people
> fall, but in an abundance of counselors
> there is safety. (Proverbs 11:14)

> A fool takes no pleasure in understand-
> ing, but only in expressing his opinion.
> (Proverbs 18:2)

The field of psychology is not the most popular. I was once asked, "What is your major?"

I said, "Psychology."

And they said, "You must not want to be successful."

I was shocked by their response. That remark did not turn me away. I wanted it even more because I understood this was not for everyone.

Another incident is when people ask me what I do for a living. In the mention of teenagers or young adults, their first response is, "I couldn't do that. You must have a lot of patience."

My response is, "Teenagers and young adults need guidance and help just like any other age group. Society has placed expectations on teenagers and young adults as if they should already know certain things; they are rude and mischievous. It's actually the opposite. Teenagers and young adults are curious, misunderstood, and trying to figure out their place in this world called life. However, I understood the assignment to be a leader, a light, and a listener to God's future generation."

My experiences as a teenager are the reason why I am so passionate about helping others, especially teenagers and young adults. I wish I had the guidance that I desire to give others. I wish I had someone who would listen without judgment. I wish I was seen for me and not my mistakes or my parents' mistakes. Now I see my life experiences weren't just for me but for me to help others who have or who are experiencing similar circumstances, to show them that they are not alone, to show them empathy, and to show them that you do not have to be perfect, just be you.

I love what I do, and I love who I am. My life is not perfect, but it is mine. When I got out of the military, I received a diamond as my plaque, and the note read, "Like a diamond, your voice cuts through everything. But you will also be remembered forever." That was a joke we had, but that diamond means so much more. I am that diamond. The process of a diamond is not easy. It goes through many steps to become the beauty that it is. The process is not beautiful, but the process is required. I have experienced many trials and tribulations to which this book can attest. I have cried more than I wanted to. I definitely did not want to experience things that I had to go through; it was a part of the process. I had to endure the process to become the person God created me to be.

I am still growing. I am still flourishing. I am still going through different processes. Now, I get it. I smile more. I live a life of gratitude. I have peace, and that's the most beautiful thing to have. I know God is still working in my life. Every day is a new beginning. The breath we take for granted; we breathe because we still have a purpose. We breathe because our assignment is not done. God has not forgotten about you. Timing is everything. In due time, you will win!

God never said that we would have peace in this world. Peace is with us because God is in us. Do not be ashamed of what you have gone through or are going through. Your light shines bright. Hold your head up high, and readjust your crown. Your Almighty God has so much in store for you!

Many times, in life, we say what we need and what we want, but we rarely say what we deserve. I deserve to be happy. You deserve to be happy. I deserve to fall in love and experience real love. You deserve to fall in love and experience real love. So allow yourself to live. Breathe and enjoy life.

And you may not be a believer in God and/or Christ. You may be a believer in science and/or the Universe. But always remember and never forget that God is the creator of *all*. He does not replicate or duplicate, and there is no one like Him. And Christ the Savior is the only one who can save you.

51

ABOUT THE AUTHOR

I am originally from Natchez, Mississippi. I received a bachelor of science in psychology with a minor in community health science from the University of Southern Mississippi. I received a master of arts in mental health counseling at Argosy University, Nashville, Tennessee. A couple of years later, I joined the military with the US Marine Corps, and I am now a proud Veteran. Recently, I received a doctor of philosophy in general psychology with an emphasis in cognition and instruction. I am appreciative of everything that I have accomplished thus far, including the challenges.

I am very passionate about psychology as it relates to helping and understanding the overall well-being. I have been in the field of psychology since 2006. I strive to provide others with the necessary skills to succeed that exemplify intrinsic and extrinsic motivation. My leadership skills are enhanced through supervising, training, counseling, and teaching others within a multicultural environment.

I have dedicated my career to helping others such as homeless women and children and emotional and behavioral children and their families. I also lead and teach our future generation in psychology. Serving the community has always been my mission as I am a Marine Corps Veteran.

I am motivated to help others. I love helping others go through the process of life and creating a better version of themselves. It's easy to settle, but don't! No one is meant to go through life alone; allow me to be there for you, to support you, to cheer you on, to help you be accountable, and to guide you! Let me encourage you! Everything is going to be okay! It's not over! Smile because victory is yours!

*May the Lord bless you and protect you. May the
Lord smile upon you and be gracious to you. May the
Lord show you His favor and give you, His peace.*
—Numbers 6:24–26